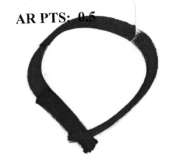

D0579820

Published in the United States of America by The Child's World®
PO Box 326 • Chanhassen, MN 55317-0326
800-599-READ • www.childsworld.com

My First Steps to Math™ is a registered trademark of Scholastic, Inc.

Library of Congress Cataloging-in-Publication Data
Moncure, Jane Belk.
My eight book / by Jane Belk Moncure.
p. cm. — (My first steps to math)
ISBN 1-59296-663-2 (lib. bdg. : alk. paper)
1. Counting—Juvenile literature. 2. Number concept—Juvenile literature. I. Title.
QA113.M66 2006
513.2'11—dc22
2005025698

My eight Book

by Jane Belk Moncure
illustrated by Paige Keiser

This is Little .

Little  lives in the house of eight.

It has eight rooms. Count them.

Every day, Little  goes for a walk.

One day, she walks
to a farm. She sees . . .

a mama hen.

Then she sees seven little yellow baby chickens . . .

pop out from under the mama's wings.
How many are in the whole family?

Little *eight* opens a gate.

She sees two brown goats,

two black goats,

and four white
goats in a pen.

Count the goats.

Little  opens the gate very wide.
How many goats run outside?

How many goats stay in the pen?

Just then the farm dog runs by.
He chases . . .

two goats

back into the pen.

Little  hops to a grapevine.
"I will pick a bunch
with eight grapes," she says.

Which bunch
does she pick?

Next Little  skips into the garden.

She picks two tomatoes,

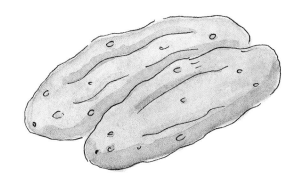

two cucumbers,

two carrots,

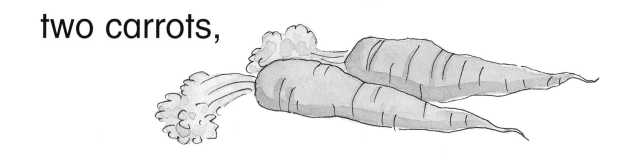

 one head of lettuce,

and one radish.

How many vegetables
does she pick in all?

"I will make a salad," she says.

Little  eight makes a very big salad.
She invites her bunny friends . . .

to a picnic.

How many bunnies come?

"Let's play hide-and-seek," says one bunny.

Little  closes her eyes.
She counts to eight
very fast. Can you?

Away hop the bunnies.

Little eight finds five bunnies

behind some bushes.

How many bunnies are still hiding?

Then Little  eight finds three bunnies

in a field
of daisies.

Has Little eight found all the bunnies?

"What pretty daisies," says Little  .
"I will give each bunny a daisy."

Little eight picks a bunch of daisies.

How many does Little eight still need?

24

The happy bunnies hop
eight hops. Can you?

Little eight hops back home.

When Little 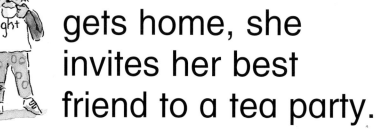 gets home, she invites her best friend to a tea party.

Little  and her friend each have a piece of cake.

How many pieces are left for you?

Little 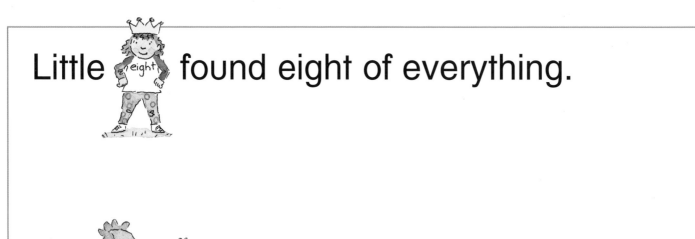 found eight of everything.

eight chickens

**eight bunches
of grapes**

eight bunnies

eight flowers

Now you find eight things.

Let's add with Little 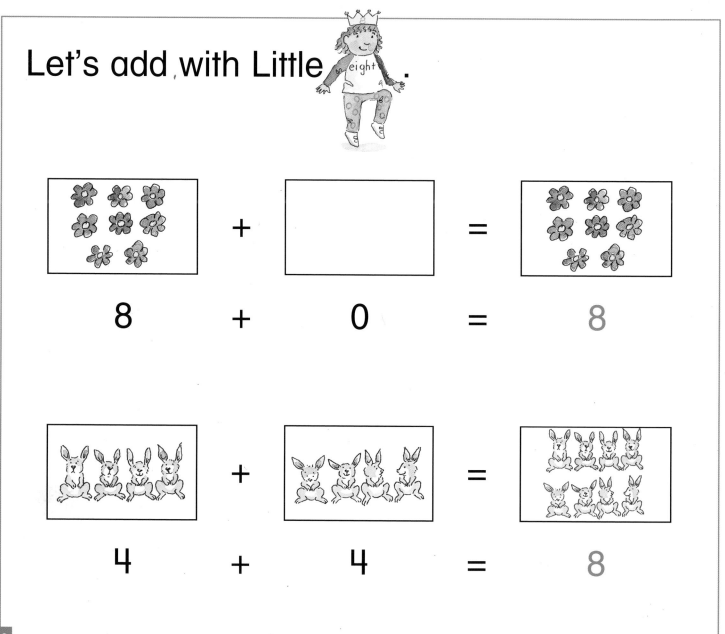 eight.

8 + 0 = 8

4 + 4 = 8

Now take away.

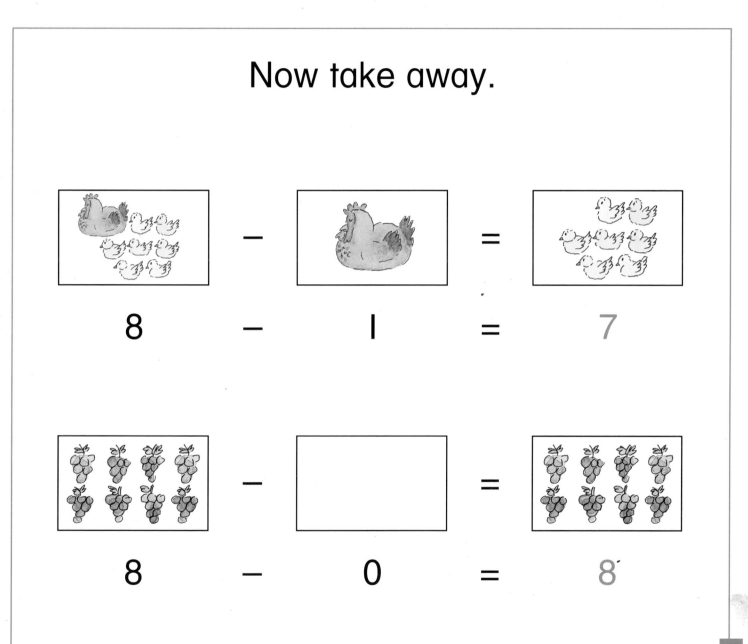

8   –   1   =   7

8   –   0   =   8

Little *eight* makes an 8 this way:

She makes the number word like this:

You can make them in the air with your finger.